A CONSUMING FIRE

DEVOTIONS FOR THE LENTEN SEASON

The Foundry Publishing
PO Box 419527
Kansas City, MO 64141
thefoundrypublishing.com

978-0-8341-4374-6

Cover design: Caines Design
Interior design: Caines Design

CONTENTS

To the Israelites the glory of the L*ORD* *looked like a consuming fire on top of the mountain.*

—Exodus 24:17

AN INVITATION TO THE JOURNEY

Before the buds of spring erupt and branches grow fistfuls of green, before the briskness of winter becomes just a memory, it is a good time to begin a heart-searching journey toward the cross and Easter. Traditionally, this time is called Lent. Lent comes from an Old English word meaning "spring." Images of new growth and new beginnings are appropriate for this season.

The journey will take forty days of soul searching. While forty isn't a magic number, it does refer to significant periods of journeying in the Bible: Jesus's forty days in the wilderness or Moses's forty days on Mount Sinai, for example. For us today, forty days offers time to set new habits and rhythms. The forty days in Lent do not count the Sundays because Sundays are for worship and celebration.

Some long-accepted practices have helped many Christians in their Lenten observances throughout history. We do not direct these practices ourselves; instead, throughout the entire season of Lent, we respond to God's nudging in order to journey and be formed in the ways that God wants from us. Let's review four common, longstanding Lenten practices.

1. Fasting

This is about soul cleaning. Ask yourself: *What can I do without so that God has more of me?* Many spiritual leaders counsel us to go beyond food. Fast from complaining, blaming, impatience, sarcasm, busyness, worry, and a slew of other soul-squatting postures that don't help us hear and follow God. (See the Beginner's Guide to Fasting beyond Food on page 9 for additional ideas.)

2. Confession and Repentance

We confess excuses that do not help us or heal us. We agree with God that some attitude or action of ours does not belong. We name it and turn away from it by God's direction and empowerment.

3. Prayer

Engaging in any spiritual activity without prayer is an exercise in futility. Without God's analysis and correction, we perpetuate self-help. Lent is a time to find different ways and rhythms to incorporate more prayer into our lives. When we endeavor to make prayer more of a dialogue than a monologue, we have a better chance of hearing God more often.

4. Service

What happens internally must show up externally somewhere. Be ready for God to deploy you. Maybe he will guide you to serve your family with more sensitivity. Maybe he will guide you to someone who needs encouragement. Volunteer somewhere new. Spiritual growth without investing it where God needs you is self-serving.

A Consuming Fire is designed to nudge spiritual awareness and growth. Yet we know that spiritual insight is not automatic. Each weekday shares a scriptural reflection, questions to help you apply the truth, an affirmation that summarizes the daily principle, and a one-sentence prayer as your commission for the day. Avoid the temptation to read the reflection without prayerfully asking yourself the questions. Don't try to answer the questions all at once. Live with them until an answer surfaces. Be intentional about obeying what God shows you.

The Sundays will encourage you to set your spiritual intention and direction for the week. Nothing propels us into our week better than worshiping the God who created us, called us, and transforms us as we do the work.

This book can be used for individual study, but consider the richness that might result from using it in community with others. Small groups could use a combination of material from the book (like the Burning Questions) as well as the small group discussion guide from the Pastor's Resource in order to propel discussion. Invite your Sunday school class to join you on this journey. It would be easy to take five minutes at the beginning of class to share an insight from the week. Suggest long-distance friends or family join you in reading the book together through the season of Lent, sharing thoughts back and forth by phone, text, or social media.

These forty days are critical to helping us learn what the cross and resurrection mean in our lives. Let God burn away what doesn't belong in your heart. Then your heart can burn bright and clean for all God wants you to know and do through Jesus and the cross.

Sharing the journey with you!

DEBBIE GOODWIN
Roswell, Georgia

A PRAYER FOR THE JOURNEY

Lord of good journeys, your heart burned with the will of your Father in a way that challenges me as well as scares me. Today, I present my heart to you, that you will create a burning in my heart that will empower me to live your will in my changing and restless world. I come ready to listen to your heart that burns for me in ways I have not understood but desperately need. Amen.

A BEGINNER'S GUIDE TO

FASTING BEYOND FOOD

Priorities

- **Keep it simple.** Instead of attempting to tackle a whole host of character flaws, choose one small indulgence, time-wasting activity, or problematic attitude to focus on this season. Remember that Lent comes around every year, and you don't have to attack all of your weaknesses at once.

- **Make it *challenging* but *achievable*.** You know yourself best. Be realistic about what you can handle. Do you want to focus on fasting once a week? Three times each week? Every day? Choose a frequency that you can achieve but that will still challenge you.

- **Engage an accountability partner.** Tell someone you trust what you are trying to do. Check in at least once a week. Tell them honestly about whether you met your goal and what you learned because of your fast.

Examples

Although biblical fasting appears to be restricted to food, fasting can take many forms. The purpose of fasting is to create space to listen to God more, or to have more time or motivation to do something for God. If fasting from food doesn't work for you, consider these ideas about other things we can fast from, especially during the season of Lent. Remember that fasting doesn't always mean that the thing we are fasting from is bad. Fasting from food doesn't mean food is bad! Food is a necessary part of our lives! Sometimes, however, engaging in a fast, even from something that is good or necessary, can help us see where we have allowed a certain thing to dominate or control our lives in unhealthy ways.

Attitudes: Let go of criticism, negativity, argument, control, selfishness, or complaining.

Activities: Give up a favorite TV show or video game. Give up shopping for fun and stick to necessities only. Take a break from activities that take you away from your family.

Creature Comforts: If you are used to using a dishwasher, choose a time (once a day, once a week, a couple times a week, etc.) to wash dishes by hand; use the extra time to pray for your family. Or consider other gadgets/appliances in your home that bring you convenience and whether you can go without them or perform those tasks the old-fashioned way. Often these practices cultivate awareness and gratitude.

Making Excuses: Learn to take responsibility for anything you did or didn't do that caused a problem for someone else (even if you didn't *mean* to cause a problem).

Expectations: Stop setting your own expectations and give God room to show you something else.

Convenient Parking Spaces: If you are able-bodied and healthy, practice servanthood by leaving good parking spaces for someone else and parking farther away from where you're going.

Gossip: Don't share information that does not build someone up.

Noise: If you are the type of person who uses the TV or music as background noise without really paying attention to it, turn off the excess noise in your life. Listen for birds or other sounds of the world existing around you. Listen for God.

Phone: Put your phone away and/or on silent when you are with friends or family, especially when gathering for a meal.

Possessions: Each week of Lent, go through a room, a closet, or a cabinet. What are you not using that someone else could? Make a plan to donate what you can part with.

Social Media: Many find that taking a break from the negativity on social media is helpful, and encourages us to reject negative postures if/when we return to social media.

Lack of Gratitude: When something happens you don't want, ask God to show you what he will do with it. What he does, if we pay attention, usually leads to gratitude.

Place in Line: Try giving up your place in a line to a stranger. Or let someone merge or get in front of you in traffic. Yield to a bicyclist, or don't rush to drive past one in a shared lane. Consider how it makes you feel to give up your own space for someone you don't even know.

Be creative! You know your own life and rhythms and routines. You know where you tend to waste time and what activities or attitudes are unhealthy for you. Pray about how God might want to transform you in this season. More often than not, God will nudge you in the direction you need to go, if you pay attention.

ASH WEDNESDAY

A BURNING IN MY HEART

SCRIPTURE

I sit in dust and ashes to show my repentance.

—Job 42:6b (NLT)

Today we begin a purposeful journey to the cross. We pray that we will receive everything God intends with the gift of his Son, Jesus. Without him, we are paupers unnecessarily. We can't give ourselves a pep talk worthy of the journey we need to make. We must come before God and humbly acknowledge that we are emptier than we want to be and weaker than we should be. We need a fresh coal of fire in our hearts that begins to blaze for what God wants to do in us, through us, and for us. We want to burn with a desire to grow in Christ.

Fire is merciless. When fire burns something, nothing is left but ashes. Perhaps that is why the first Wednesday of this forty-day journey to the cross begins with an object lesson involving ashes. Whatever God says does not belong in our hearts must burn away to leave only ashes. Additionally, ashes also remind us of how temporary our lives are.

Many attend an Ash Wednesday service where the pastor makes a cross with ashes on the foreheads of those who gather. The metaphor has its roots in the Old Testament, where ashes were sprinkled on the heads of people who mourned a predicament only God could solve. The ashes represented their helplessness.

This humbling is necessary. Until we admit we are not self-made, we cannot stand before the cross to receive what God says we need. Humbling ourselves is the gutting of every excuse and rationalization. It is the detoxification of what our culture pushes on us. We need this slow, soulful journey to the cross because our hearts carry weights and chaos that God never intended us to experience. We remember who we are and who we are not. We bring our unedited selves to God so he can burn away what does not need to stay. When God does his work, a new burning begins in our hearts, and we wait, humbled and ready to listen.

BURNING QUESTIONS

1. What must burn away so that God has complete access to my goals, motives, and actions?

____

____

____

____

2. Where does God want me to use his power?

3. What commitment will help me make the most of this devotional journey?

AFFIRMATION

I was created for life with God.

PRAYER FOR TODAY

Eternal God, burn away what does not help me see you, hear you, or obey you.

THURSDAY

HAVE MERCY

SCRIPTURE

Have mercy on me, O God, according to your unfailing love; according to your great compassion blot out my transgressions.

—Psalm 51:1

We are not quick mercy givers in the United States. Our courts aren't known for giving mercy, and our corporate and political systems distribute even less. Instead, power rules. The more power, the better, and mercy is locked out.

I have learned that the prayer that frees God to do his best work in my life is a prayer for mercy. Requesting God's mercy says we do not understand enough to know what we should ask. Or we recognize how deep our need is and know that only what God chooses will address it.

I learned this lesson best as I prayed for our daughter, who lived with complicated and disabling physical and learning issues. More than once I cried, "Have mercy on us!" I learned that what God brought when I prayed for mercy answered a need I didn't recognize. God's mercy met my deepest need instead of answering a surface issue that didn't go deep enough.

As we present our hearts to God, let's ask for his mercy. Nothing clears the way for us to hear from God more than confessing our need for him and what he chooses for us. His mercy connects us to his unfailing love. Knowing how much we are loved, our hearts burn with a new fire to return his love as obedience, which is always the best response to God's mercy.

BURNING QUESTIONS

1. Who has hurt me, and whom have I hurt?

2. Where do I need mercy, and with whom should I share mercy?

AFFIRMATION

God is closer than my heartbeat and always ready to share his mercy.

PRAYER FOR TODAY

Merciful Lord, have mercy on me when I am overwhelmed,
helpless, or have not received mercy from others.

FRIDAY

NO MORE HIDING

SCRIPTURE

For I know my transgressions, and my sin is always before me.

—Psalm 51:3

David is confessing his sin against Bathsheba and God. David tried to ignore that he had done something against God. He wouldn't admit his wrong motives and actions. He was hiding. I imagine him during those days as a worried, troubled man who was sick of himself and more afraid than he admitted. He knew what he did. He could hide it from people, but he couldn't hide it from God.

God came looking for David using the prophet Nathan. At first, David felt exposed and found out. Instead, David had been *found*. It was the beginning of his restoration.

We hide so much from others, thinking that what doesn't show, doesn't matter. But it does matter because we were not made for hiding. We were created for honesty, openness, and intimacy. Hiding brings lies. Live with lies long enough, and they become our truths.

Since God already knows the truth, we only play hide and seek with ourselves. It's easier to rationalize our words and actions to excuse ourselves or blame someone else. However, God sees through our futile attempts to hide the truth. He waits for us to stop hiding. Then he does not give a reprimand; he shows us the way to restoration. Big or little, it doesn't matter as much as refusing to hide whatever it was.

Repeat after me: No. More. Hiding.

BURNING QUESTIONS

1. What excuses do I use to hide what I don't want to admit?

2. How can I be more honest with myself? With God?

AFFIRMATION

Since God is honest with me, I need to be honest with God.

PRAYER FOR TODAY

Affirming Father, help me reject the temptation to hide what you want to address so I can enjoy the kind of intimacy with you where no hiding is needed.

SATURDAY

JUST COME

SCRIPTURE

Come to me, all you who are weary and burdened, and I will give you rest.

—Matthew 11:28

Rest is the biggest unmet need in our get-it-done culture. We push and exhaust ourselves with the useless goal of finishing what we think we need to get done.

Jesus isn't inviting us to a nap—at least not most of the time. He is inviting us to hear his heart. He whispers this invitation. Maybe that's why we don't hear it—because it gets drowned out by louder voices.

At the beginning of this journey to the cross, we must be more determined to follow his ways. For example, Jesus was never in a hurry. Interruptions didn't throw him off. He accepted them as part of his Father's gifts of the day. He was present for people who needed him. He didn't multitask or overthink productivity.

When Jesus asks us to turn over our troubled minds—including our can't-finish lists—to him, what prevents us from obeying? What has such a hold on us that we aren't eager to answer this invitation? Are we so enslaved to productivity that we add Jesus's call to the end of our list, in case we have time to spare? Isn't that backward?

Find one day to turn it around. Start your day by giving Jesus everything that has you uptight and worried. Let Jesus rest you with his commanding peace and presence. Then go into your day, letting him give you one task at a time.

Just come. His invitation will never go away until you do.

BURNING QUESTIONS

1. What part of Jesus's invitation speaks to you today?

2. How will you answer him?

AFFIRMATION

Jesus has rest for me. All I must do is come.

PRAYER FOR TODAY

Ever-speaking Jesus, help me ignore any voice—especially my own—that prevents me from answering your invitation.

FIRST SUNDAY IN LENT

A BURNING INVITATION

WORSHIP FOCUS

Just come!

SCRIPTURE

Come, let us bow down in worship, let us kneel before the LORD *our Maker.*

—Psalm 95:6

What increases our desire for everything God wants to give us?

What makes us recognize how God delights in rescuing us from a self-reliance that will never save us?

What understanding, gratitude, or obedience will this realization birth?

This week, listen for God's voice. It will be the most encouraging, directing, and loving voice. Let whatever God shares become the spark to ignite a burning in your heart for what God wants to give.

BURNING QUESTION

How will you prepare to be present for God in worship?

____

____

____

____

____

____

____

____

____

____

____

____

____

____

SUNDAY PRAYER

Gracious Lord, I will answer your invitation to be present for you because you are always present for me.

MONDAY

RETURN TO ME

SCRIPTURE

"Even now," declares the LORD, "return to me with all your heart, with fasting and weeping and mourning."

—Joel 2:12

No voice should ever take priority over God's voice. However, we often prefer our own thoughts and perspectives, even as we long to hear what God has to say. God's invitation to return to him is crucial because God invites us to return to who he knows we can be in him and by him.

We return to the God who made us. We return to the One who knows more about us than any parent, spouse, or friend. We return to the One whose hopes for us are not far-fetched or impossible. We return to the One who can rest us in the deepest place of our weariness.

As we take our journey to the cross, we rest first. Rest from every undone task, every unmet goal, every pushy voice in our heads. Rest from disappointments and pain. Just rest.

Let the One who created you renew your belief in his unfailing love and unending resources. When you know where true rest waits, your hungry heart will help you find it. Rest becomes the first gift of this journey.

BURNING QUESTIONS

1. What practice or routine helps you return to God with all your heart?

2. What do you need to rest from in order to hear God better?

3. How will you practice resting today?

AFFIRMATION

God calls me to return to him with a hunger for everything he wants to say and supply.

PRAYER FOR TODAY

Gentle Lord, I need your rest today. I will listen more than talk when I pray.

TUESDAY

COME FASTING

SCRIPTURE

Come fasting and weeping, sorry for your sins!
Change your life, not just your clothes.

—Joel 2:12b–13a (MSG)

We don't like to do without things. We live in a culture that pushes getting more in every category we can think of.

But the call to the cross is to set something aside that our heart does not need, in order that we may grow. God invites us to get rid of whatever makes it hard to hear what God is saying, whether that's an appetite, a habit, an action, a relationship, or an attitude. We call this fasting. Lent is a good time to get used to living without something we don't need. We replace what we remove with something we need even more—time with God.

In our contemporary mindset, we think more about multitasking than reducing. However, God doesn't call us to get more done. He calls us to accomplish the right things. We need to listen to the voice that brings God's peace. We need this time to clear the clutter and listen to God better.

Although there will always be busy seasons, life should never be characterized as one busy season after another. Fasting makes time for the God who always makes time for us. Fasting helps us return to unforced and uncomplicated time with God, where he has more to say than we do.

BURNING QUESTIONS

1. What can you do without that will create the time you need with God?

2. What is stunting your spiritual growth that you can do without?

AFFIRMATION

Because God always makes time for me, I will make time for God.

PRAYER FOR TODAY

Abundant Giver, help me to do without what I do not need so I have more of your abundance.

WEDNESDAY

INTO THE WILDERNESS

SCRIPTURE

Jesus, full of the Holy Spirit, left the Jordan
and was led by the Spirit into the wilderness.

—Luke 4:1

Some translations of this scripture say "desert" instead of "wilderness." My personal deserts aren't hot, sandy expanses where a merciless sun threatens and thirst could kill me. My deserts are places where I feel alone in all the wrong ways. Illness that drags on or a recovery that doesn't go fast enough can be a desert. Moving to a new place where you don't know anyone and aren't known can be a desert.

How we handle our deserts usually depends on whom we listen to when we experience them. Isolation can play tricks on us. Yet isolation also gets us away from crowds and activities that keep us from hearing God. Deserts give us the opportunity to listen to the right voice. Because it is not usually the loudest voice, we must choose wisely.

Jesus started his ministry with a trip to the desert, where only three voices existed: his, his Father's, and the tempter's. Jesus refuted the tempter's voice. When he did, the voice of his Father became the only voice he wanted to hear.

Don't get caught in a tug-of-war between the put-downs and unnecessary questions of the wrong voice. Don't assume that self-talk is always true. Instead, listen for the voice that settles you with an affirmation you would never give yourself. Listen for the voice that speaks with hope for what you can do and be. Then, just as Jesus left his desert with new resolve for his mission, you will too.

BURNING QUESTIONS

1. Where or when have you experienced a desert? What voice did you hear first?

2. What helps you hear and recognize God's voice in the desert? How can you practice today?

AFFIRMATION

As God speaks in my desert, I will do what it takes to recognize his voice quickly.

PRAYER FOR TODAY

Speak, Lord, for your servant is listening.

THURSDAY

TEMPTED

SCRIPTURE

Then Jesus was led by the Spirit into the wilderness to be tempted by the devil.

—Matthew 4:1 NIV

When Jesus was tempted in the wilderness, he used his experience to settle the trajectory of his life and confirm his mission to be the bridge to bring people to his Father. False accusations didn't distract him. Debate didn't unnerve him. Misunderstanding and betrayal from his followers didn't make him question the mission. Jesus's focus on his Father in the wilderness strengthened how he embraced his mission, and nothing made him lose focus.

I vacillate more than I would like. I speak confidently about faith in God, try to teach it clearly, and still wonder if I am choosing right in life situations. Questions haunt me like day-old garlic bread. In those times, I ask the wrong questions. I want specifics about the time and place when God wants to give me my next step of obedience. Yet I need to remember how Jesus responded to temptation.

Jesus took the Word of his Father and used it as his shield to reject the lies and empty promises of the tempter. And then he feasted—not on bread, or power. He feasted on every word from his Father.

When we know that God has our best interests at heart and will do anything to kindle a fire in our hearts for what he wants, we feast there too.

BURNING QUESTIONS

1. What has temptation taught you about yourself?

2. How might God want to prepare a feast for you in your wilderness?

AFFIRMATION

God will always empower me with what I need to reject temptation.

PRAYER FOR TODAY

Always-present God, help me practice listening to your voice instead of the tempter's voice.

FRIDAY

HUNGER AND THIRST

SCRIPTURE

Blessed are those who hunger and thirst for righteousness, for they will be filled.

—*Matthew 5:6*

Many of us live in a culture that doesn't understand thirst. So many of us have known only the kind of periodic hunger that can be immediately sated, rather than the kind of gnawing, painful hunger that persists because there is literally no food. Many of us carry bottled water and snacks with us everywhere, or we are usually capable of getting food and water whenever we need or want it. But what about a hunger and thirst for all that God wants us to know and do? How do we recognize that kind of hunger? We have trouble addressing what we don't experience.

Reconnecting with what Jesus did for us is why we take this journey to the cross. This careful review reminds us that Jesus didn't just save us; he continues to fill us. We become even more hungry and thirsty for God's Word and his Spirit of truth. When we stay hungry and thirsty for God, we will be invited to a need-meeting oasis where God shares a truth or makes his presence known. When he does, it only makes us hunger and thirst for more, and that becomes our motivation for growth.

Without a gnawing hunger and eager thirst, we revert to try-harder growth techniques that will eventually fail because they come from misunderstandings about where growth originates. Jesus calls us to follow *him.* It is a call to grow into the person God knows we can be. Follow his nudges—especially the ones that come from his Word. Then you will always hunger and thirst for more.

BURNING QUESTIONS

1. How can you recognize your hunger and thirst for God today?

2. How will you identify and make time for God's oasis for you today?

AFFIRMATION

God fills the hungry with good things.

PRAYER FOR TODAY

Helpful Lord, I need your help to recognize my hunger and thirst for you before you can meet that need.

SATURDAY

DON'T FORGET

SCRIPTURE

You forget the LORD your Maker, who stretches out the heavens and who lays the foundations of the earth.

—Isaiah 51:13a

How often does someone remind us: Don't forget the milk, your lunch, to pick up the kids, or some other task? Do reminders sear the instruction in special memory cells of our brains? Not unless we do something like write a note, set an alarm, or take care of the issue immediately. We are prone to forget if we don't do something that will help us remember.

Isaiah is full of reminders to the people of God who were exiled because of what they forgot. They forgot who God called them to be. They forgot how to live in God's way. Forgetting made them complain. Forgetting made them entitled. Forgetting created a distance that God never wanted.

Did you know the word "remember" is used more than 1,200 times in the Bible? God knows we need reminding. He is diligent about keeping his truth before us. But we forget. We get busy or distracted or tired. We complain that our brains don't hold enough. Yet science tells us that our brains are underused.

We need a daily dose of remembering who God is, what he is

doing for us, and what he wants from us. We must remember we are not self-made. We were created for a purpose. Most of all, we were made for a relationship with God. Pleasing him first is a good way to remember what he wants in other areas of our lives. God invites us to remember him so we stay ready to hear his encouragement, direction, warning, and love.

Don't forget who God is and who he wants to be in your life. Be specific. Be eager. Be his. Then forgetting will be harder than trying to remember.

BURNING QUESTIONS

1. How will you remember to live in God's way in this generation and culture?

2. How does remembering God as your Maker and Sustainer remove your need to complain?

AFFIRMATION

As I remember who God is and what he has done for me, I will enjoy a deeper relationship with him.

PRAYER FOR TODAY

Lord of perfect memory, help me remember who you are and whose I am.

SECOND SUNDAY IN LENT

A BURNING NEED

WORSHIP FOCUS

Yearning

SCRIPTURE

My soul yearns, even faints, for the courts of the Lord;
my heart and my flesh cry out for the living God.

—Psalm 84:2

God is generous in ways we will never understand. He has promised to meet our needs, and he also blesses us with surprises. Too often we elevate our wants to needs. We fear we won't get what we want otherwise. It is a useless game because God recognizes our childish wordplay. Instead, God prioritizes meeting needs because, when he satisfies a need, it often satisfies a want even better.

This week, let's allow God's need-meeting history to help us understand how insufficient our ideas about our needs are. Let's find out what God gives because of what we need.

BURNING QUESTION

What does your heart yearn for that God wants to give you today?

SUNDAY PRAYER

Loving God, I will be open to what you say I need before I tell you what I think I need.

MONDAY

AN ACCOUNTING

SCRIPTURE

What will I do when God confronts me?
What will I answer when called to account?

—Job 31:14

Few people look forward to annual reviews, regardless of whether the evaluation is medical or professional. We're afraid we may not pass some sort of test. When someone else holds the power to change our lives with a review, it can be scary. Lent is a good time for a spiritual review. We can ask God, "How am I doing?" The good news is that God is often kinder and more affirming than we tend to be with ourselves.

Because of the cross, we start with what Christ did for us and ask God to evaluate how we live because of his unbelievable sacrifice. We examine ourselves against Christ's performance. Our culture doesn't teach us to review this way. Instead, it must be a deliberate choice. We are called to answer life-giving questions: *Do we love with God's love? Do we serve with humble joy? Do we worry unnecessarily about what God promised to take care of? Are we cooperating with God's timing?*

To answer these questions honestly, we look at Jesus's life first. Then we ask God to help us find the same seamless, intimate, and transformative relationship Jesus had with his Father. We pray the Gethsemane prayer: *your will, not mine*. We keep praying this prayer until it is true in the small and large choices. We pray the prayer until God's will becomes the only way to satisfy the burning need in our hearts.

While we are called to give an account, we are not called to cower in fear of a reprimand. We are called to enjoy God's welcome and delight as he directs our transformation. When his joy becomes ours, we no longer fear what we give up because what he provides is more than enough to satisfy our burning needs.

BURNING QUESTIONS

1. What do you hear when you ask God, "How am I doing?"

2. What do you discover about your spiritual accounting when you use the questions from today's reflection?

AFFIRMATION

The One who called me to follow him will lead my review with love and affirmation.

PRAYER FOR TODAY

Truthful Lord, I come to you for accountability and review. My life is open and ready.

TUESDAY

ALL MY NEEDS

SCRIPTURE

And my God will meet all your needs according to the riches of his glory in Christ Jesus.

—Philippians 4:19

Can God really meet *all* our needs? Paul, the writer of the letter to the Philippian church, is the true poster child for allowing God to define and meet needs. He testified to accessing glorious riches in Christ that met everything he needed. I am glad God doesn't give me everything I *say* I need. He knows more than I do and refuses to shortchange me by working within my boundaries. Instead, he offers his wisdom from his all-knowing perspective.

What riches do we receive? One that I value is being rescued from depending on our best efforts to save ourselves or to grow spiritually by trying harder. God works in us through his Spirit by a whisper, a nudge, or a background voice we learn to recognize and give priority to. And that's just for starters.

As we continue our journey to the cross, keep listening for his invitation. He invites us to his heart. He wants us close enough to hear when he speaks. He wants us to recognize the depth of his unfailing love no matter the question. When we accept his invitation to come, listen, or obey, the right answers to real needs will follow.

BURNING QUESTIONS

1. How do you tell the difference between a need and a want?

2. Why do you have trouble trusting that God knows your needs better than you do?

AFFIRMATION

God is a need-meeting God and knows my needs better than I do.

PRAYER FOR THE DAY

Generous Giver, protect me from misunderstanding my needs
so I can recognize how you meet all I need.

WEDNESDAY

MORE GRACE

SCRIPTURE

But he gives us more grace.

—James 4:6a

We always need more of something: money, closeness in relationships, sleep. I usually need more time. I often put more on my to-do list than I can reasonably finish, and then I pat myself on the back when I accomplish half of my list.

I am slowly learning that God's list for me is shorter and more focused. God reminds us that he is the first *more* of anything we need. He has a long list of what he will give more of if we ask. He loves giving more insight, discernment, courage, restraint, and wisdom (see Philippians 1:9). Often we don't ask for what he says we can have more of, and then we live with unmet needs unnecessarily.

God has never changed a clock to give us more time. He won't tell the dark to wait a little longer so we can get more done. But he will give us more focus. He will help us set good priorities. He will give us what we need to accomplish his will. If God's *more* isn't enough to complete what we need to do, maybe we should listen more closely and make fewer lists.

BURNING QUESTIONS

1. Where do you need more of God's insight to set today's priorities?

2. Where do you need to ask more from God before you ask for more of anything else?

AFFIRMATION

My resourceful God knows how to give me what I need the most.

PRAYER FOR TODAY

God of more, choose what I need more of today
so that I may experience your incomparable more!

THURSDAY

I WANT TO SEE

SCRIPTURE

"What do you want me to do for you?" Jesus asked him. The blind man said, "Rabbi, I want to see."

—Mark 10:51

When our daughter began to lose her eyesight, her world changed. She could still see light, but it wasn't enough. Shapes lost their edges, and faces ran together. Words drowned on pages without hope of rescue. What she couldn't see with her eyes, she began to see with her ears and her heart. She learned that sight was a whole-body experience.

Jesus understood that sight is more than a function of the eyes alone. He spoke against the unnecessary blindness that had disabled his church family. He called Pharisees "blind guides" (Matthew 23:16). It was self-inflicted blindness. They couldn't see who Jesus was because they *wouldn't* see.

Where is our blindness today? Where are we quick to point a finger at someone else's sin and pat ourselves on the back with pharisaical arrogance, thinking, *I am not like them*? Pride can make us blind much more quickly than disease can. What if we used this journey to the cross to ask Jesus to help us see better? How could we use our sight to look at ourselves through God's eyes and not just our own? The healing of a blind heart is harder than the healing of physical blindness. We see what we want to see without processing the deficit.

In a hopeful story, a stumbling blind man pushed through the crowd to get to Jesus.

"What do you want me to do for you?" Jesus asked the blind man.

"I want to see."

Jesus answered his cry, and a whole new world burst into color and nuance before him. We need to ask Jesus for the same world-opening sight.

BURNING QUESTIONS

1. Where do you have difficulty seeing others as Jesus sees them?

____

____

____

____

____

____

____

____

____

____

____

2. Where are you blind to your own faults but quick to point out faults in others?

AFFIRMATION

Jesus can heal my heart's blindness if I ask.

PRAYER FOR TODAY

Lord of perfect vision, open the eyes of my heart,
that I may see myself and the world as you see them.

FRIDAY

FATHER KNOWS BEST

SCRIPTURE

Your Father knows what you need before you ask him.

—Matthew 6:8b

In the television program *Father Knows Best* that aired in the 1950s, the character Jim Anderson seemed to always know the right words to say or the best advice to give. We knew it was just a show with a written script and actors, but sometimes we wished it was true. We wanted Jim Anderson for our own dad.

Today we can live a different version of that show because we have a Father who always knows best. He knows what we need and the best time to give it. He knows what we try to hide, and he would rather forgive us than shame us. He knows we are worth more than we think we are. He wants a chance to prove it to us, but sometimes we listen instead to the lies people use to wound us. Or sometimes we stubbornly cling to who we think we are and what we need. Other times we fear that someone may push us down if we don't push them first.

We need to stop pretending that we know best. We must live

in the protection of knowing that our Father knows best, gives best, and loves best. He knows what overwhelms, scares, limits, or breaks us. He uses what he knows to give us what we need. Until we stop pretending we know best, we won't come to God with open hearts to allow him to work from the inside out. We won't be ready for what he wants to give.

Today, live your life in the knowledge that our Father knows best. Find out how he gives what we need even when we don't know how to ask for it. Look for the ways he supplies something that helps more than we could imagine. Let it make you more grateful for having a Father who knows best.

BURNING QUESTIONS

1. How does your life demonstrate that God knows you best?

2. Where do you deny that God knows best?

3. How does God's knowledge about you shape how you pray and what you ask for?

AFFIRMATION

God knows more about me than I know about myself.

PRAYER FOR TODAY

Need-meeting God, thank you for supplying what I need even if it isn't what I expected or thought I wanted.

SATURDAY

WE NEED MORE HOPE

SCRIPTURE

He has delivered us from such a deadly peril, and he will deliver us again. On him we have set our hope that he will continue to deliver us.

—2 Corinthians 1:10

We live in a hopeless culture. Post-pandemic, we have lost what we believed would never change. We understand "tentative" in a way we never wanted to. We've collected more maybes about a future we can't predict. We've also collected more fears. What we believed was permanent and untouchable has slipped through our fingers.

We need hope that is firm and unchanging. It won't come from our culture, our politicians, or our protests. It comes the same way it came more than two thousand years ago—from God's great gift through Jesus. God didn't send Jesus to us as a theory, a construct, or a premise. Hope came as a *person* to be our only unchanging hope in a changing world. God knew we couldn't live victoriously in this broken world without hope, so he planted his hope in us when we joined the family of the redeemed. We must allow his hope to grow like a stem looking for light. Then this gift becomes a lifeline. Living in his hope means that nothing happens to us or around us that can steal our unfailing hope.

How can we rediscover how the hope that Jesus brought changes our perspective and influences our attitudes? How can God's hope help us stand firm in our broken world? We fix our eyes on Jesus instead of the bad news on television because God's got the whole world in his hands. We remember to live the promise that God will meet all our needs because God's got us! We wait for the answer he brings because God's got our future! We rehearse the truth that the One who lives in us is greater than anything or anyone in the world. That's hope with a capital H, and we find that hope nowhere else but in Jesus.

God's people should be hope carriers who demonstrate what it looks like to live in hope, no matter the circumstances. The world will still look dark. Yet if we can be a candle of hope and put all our candles together, we can make our corner of the world brighter.

BURNING QUESTIONS

1. How can you live with eternal hope in today's changing world?

2. Who needs you to be a carrier of hope in order to share where your hope comes from?

AFFIRMATION

I can share hope in my world as God shares his hope with me.

PRAYER FOR TODAY

God of all hope, empower me to share your hope anywhere I sense hopelessness.

THIRD SUNDAY IN LENT

A BURNING DESIRE

WORSHIP FOCUS

Desiring God First

SCRIPTURE

And I will make an everlasting covenant with them:
I will never stop doing good for them.
I will put a desire in their hearts to worship me,
and they will never leave me.

—Jeremiah 32:40 (NLT)

God wants to accomplish a spring cleaning in our hearts as we take this thoughtful journey to the cross. This cleaning involves God's examination of our hearts—where motives begin, attitudes develop, and perspectives rule.

Why begin there? Because our actions and words come from them. When we submit to the cleaning God desires, we find that submission is more about what we gain than what we lose. Submission connects us to a burning desire to do God's will.

BURNING QUESTION

How do I describe the desire God has placed in my heart for this day of worship?

____

____

____

____

____

____

____

____

____

____

____

____

____

SUNDAY PRAYER

Reviewer of my heart, deepen my desire for your examination.

MONDAY

LETTING GO

SCRIPTURE

So humble yourselves under the mighty power of God,
and at the right time he will lift you up in honor.
Give all your worries and cares to God, for he cares about you.

—1 Peter 5:6–7 (NLT)

One morning I was listening to a piano solo on my music app. The melody called to me. Usually, I don't pay attention to song titles, but something about the gentle runs and rhythm of this particular song had me looking for more information. I looked at the title: "Letting Go." It was my invitation for that morning. I leaned my head back, closed my eyes, and listened.

"What do I need to let go of?" I asked God. Don't ask if you don't want to know. Immediately the list rolled in front of me. There were concerns about our daughter's vision loss, my professional future, all the changes of the past year, and the changes that waited in the future. All were things I couldn't control or plan for.

Let it go. That's when I knew it wasn't the music speaking. It was God speaking my heart language. *Let it go. I've got this. All of it. I've got you. I've got here. I've got tomorrow. Just let go.*

Then I realized how much I carried unnecessarily. Fear, no matter how logical, does not lead to trust. Trust is possible when it's anchored in the unchanging, unfailing, all-knowing, and securing power of God. With a couple of sighs, I did it. First in my head, then in my heart.

There is no permanent "let go" trick or formula. We all need reminders. However, the best reason for letting go is what waits on the other side of surrender: God's heart-stilling peace is my security system, and worry is the intruder to be arrested. When we are ready to do anything for his peace, we will let go of anything that prevents it. Is today your day to let go?

BURNING QUESTIONS

1. What do you carry that you need to let go of?

2. How can you make surrendering to God your doorway to peace?

AFFIRMATION

I have peace when I know that God can handle my concerns better than I can carry them.

PRAYER FOR TODAY

God of true peace, help me put my worries in your capable hands today.

TUESDAY

FINDING HOME

SCRIPTURE

Do not conform to the pattern of this world, but be transformed by the renewing of your mind. Then you will be able to test and approve what God's will is—his good, pleasing and perfect will.

—Romans 12:2

I love the GPS "go home" command. It means that, no matter how lost I feel, there is a way home, and GPS will take me there. Don't you wish GPS could help us find God's will too? Even though it won't, God does provide us with his special version of GPS assistance. Jesus told us that he would share his "Spirit of truth," who would "guide you into all the truth" (John 16:13). The Holy Spirit is our guide to God's will. To know God's will, we need to recognize how the Holy Spirit is the truest voice in our minds to show us God's will, which is the truth for any circumstance.

Sometimes the Holy Spirit nudges through something like an internal whisper. Sometimes the Spirit points to an action we need to take. Sometimes the Spirit brings Scripture into our minds to help us recognize and choose God's will.

We also must connect God's character to his will. One of my spiritual mentors said, "God is more than who you think he is;

but who you think he is affects how you respond to him." We need an accurate understanding of God's character because God will not affirm anything that does not represent his character as defined in his Word.

When we ask God to live in us, he plants a hunger for his will that we must nurture. We nurture this hunger with every step of obedience. Sometimes multiple small obediences teach us more about God's will than one big obedience. For example, taking responsibility for words that hurt or do not strengthen a relationship could be a step of obedience that restores or protects a relationship.

If the word "will" confuses you, pray for God's wisdom. It's the same thing. What God wills for us is wise beyond our knowing. It is always easier to know God's will when we want his will more than ours, when his will is more adventure than duty, more "want to" than "ought to." Then his will becomes our hope, our safe place, and our heart's home, where God always waits with a welcome.

BURNING QUESTIONS

1. How have you struggled to know God's will, or where have you been afraid to ask for it?

____

____

____

____

____

2. How will you live God's will today?

AFFIRMATION

Recognizing and obeying God's will is my best way to be at peace with God.

PRAYER FOR TODAY

Lord of my life, may your good and perfect will be done in my mind, heart, and actions.

WEDNESDAY

ROOTED

SCRIPTURE

Let your roots grow down into him, and let your lives be built on him.
Then your faith will grow strong in the truth you were taught,
and you will overflow with thankfulness.

—Colossians 2:7 (NLT)

We lived in Portland, Oregon, where rain was mostly a fine mist or light shower and umbrellas were optional. Occasionally, hard rains soaked the ground, and old-growth trees without deep roots fell fast. That's the truth about roots. You don't think you need them until you do.

Jesus wants us to grow healthy roots. If our roots come from anyone or anywhere but Jesus, we begin a slow slide to a self-supported life, which may turn out to be more shallow than we think it is. Being rooted *in* Christ means everything grows from Christ's life in us, including priorities, goals, relationships, and motivation.

To be rooted in Jesus also delivers nourishment that comes from nowhere else—not from success, productivity, acceptance, or control. This is where the cross makes a difference in how we live daily. Everything we need to grow deep roots is ours as we live *in* Christ and *by* his power. We grow roots when we allow

Jesus to speak his love and truth into our lives. We grow roots when we follow his nudge to do something, say something, or be quiet. Nothing grows roots faster than obedience.

Without deep-growing roots, we will struggle, especially in hard times. We may substitute trying harder for trust in God. We will stunt our growth instead of encouraging it. We will live depleted unnecessarily. Growth is an invitation before it is a goal. It is Christ's invitation to come, listen, follow, and obey. Pray for spiritual roots, and follow God's directions for developing them. If we shortchange ourselves here, we could experience the same plight as the plant whose roots don't hold in bad weather. We may struggle, wither, and topple.

Asking for the desire to grow is a prayer God loves to answer. Don't complicate it by being an overachiever. Rooted and grounded in him—that's our focus. The life that grows from this initiative perseveres because we are rooted in the foundation of the world, the cornerstone, the eternal Christ. Nothing we try to do can substitute for what he does in us.

BURNING QUESTIONS

1. How would you describe your spiritual root system? Shallow? Beginning? Deepening?

___

___

___

___

___

2. What will grow your roots that will help you face uncertain times?

AFFIRMATION

Growth is a byproduct of obedience.

PRAYER FOR TODAY

Lord of all growth, help me recognize the difference between self-made goals and listening to your nudges to grow.

THURSDAY

LOOKING FOR SIGNS

SCRIPTURE

So we have not stopped praying for you since we first heard about you. We ask God to give you complete knowledge of his will and to give you spiritual wisdom and understanding. Then the way you live will always honor and please the Lord, and your lives will produce every kind of good fruit. All the while, you will grow as you learn to know God better and better.

—Colossians 1:9–10 (NLT)

When I drive to a new place, I look for street signs or landmarks. If I'm honest, I wish someone was waiting at an intersection with a sign that said: "This way, Debbie." Then I would know it's *my* sign. That's what we want from God too, right? We want God to give us our own sign when choices confuse us or a direction isn't clear. We want a sign to help us know for sure. Sometimes out of desperation, we grab anything that *looks* or *feels* right. Then we make our case for why this was our sign from God. But deep inside, we may still wonder.

God will give us signs, but they won't be billboards. They are more like nudges, openings, or an awareness that does not go away but grows stronger.

Peace is one of God's heart signs. Not circumstantial peace that removes whatever triggered our fear or stress. This peace comes despite distress. This peace only makes sense when we trust God for what we do not know.

Hope is another sign. God always gives us a reason to hope. We lose our way when we look for hope to show up in how we want our circumstances to be different. We find hope when we remember that God always knows what we don't. We hope for what God *will do*, not what we *want* God to do.

Timing is another sign that is easy to miss or misuse. Here we must use our spiritual eyes as our compass to look for factors that come together in ways we couldn't have made happen on our own. That's when we see God working as all the signs come together to point in the same direction.

The ultimate sign God sent us was Jesus. Jesus pointed the way to find God's will through obedience, servanthood, and surrender. It is the same path for us. Obedience teaches trust. Servanthood teaches humility. Surrender teaches authority. These are the signs that affirm God's will. What else do we need?

BURNING QUESTIONS

1. Where have you recognized God's signs of peace, hope, and timing?

____

____

____

____

____

2. Where have you missed or ignored God's signs? What was the result?

___

AFFIRMATION

God wants me to do his will and sends his signs to point the way.

PRAYER FOR TODAY

Direction-giving Lord, when I look for direction,
remind me to look for your signs to guide me.

FRIDAY

A WORD OF FAITH

SCRIPTURE

When Jesus heard this, he was amazed at him, and turning to the crowd following him, he said, "I tell you, I have not found such great faith even in Israel."

—Luke 7:9

I love the story Luke told of the centurion's faith. The centurion was a gentile asking for help from Jesus, who was Jewish. This Roman officer sent Jewish elders to deliver a message to Jesus that the officer's servant was desperately ill. Jesus, always ready to help, began walking toward the centurion's home. The centurion must have seen Jesus coming because he sent other messengers to tell Jesus to just "say the word" (Luke 7:7).

If I put myself in this story, I wouldn't be the centurion or one of the elders. I would be one of the messengers pushing Jesus to walk faster and get to the house before the servant died. That's why the centurion's faith humbles me. He only wanted a word from Jesus. But there is no record to tell us what that word was. Jesus didn't stop, raise his head toward heaven, and say, "Heal," elongating the vowels to guarantee there was no mistake about what he asked. This was a lesson about faith, not about healing!

Real faith acknowledges the presence and power of the Word made flesh. All arguments to persuade Jesus about how great the need is are unnecessary. He already knows. We want Jesus to *say the word* that brings change, healing, or help. The problem is, we don't know what that word is. But isn't that where faith comes in? Jesus knows the right word. *Say the word* becomes a simple prayer that gives Jesus all control. We don't direct; we receive. Our faith is in who Jesus is before it is in what can do. He will do whatever is right, true, best, empowering, holy, and eternal. Nothing more, nothing less.

We need faith-building experiences like the centurion had. Maybe some are waiting on the other side of our asking Jesus to send us his word for the moment, the day, or the hardship. Perhaps it's not a word with vowels and consonants because he himself is the Word. His presence means we need fewer words because we recognize the power of the Word himself.

Today, pray with confidence: *Say the word!*

BURNING QUESTIONS

1. How is it backward to connect faith to what Jesus does *for* you rather than connecting to who Jesus is?

____

____

____

____

____

____

2. How can you learn more about who Jesus is to you today?

AFFIRMATION

The Word became flesh and still speaks the word I need to hear.

PRAYER FOR TODAY

Speaking Lord, say the word I need today. If I listen more, I need fewer words.

SATURDAY

HONESTY WITH GOD

SCRIPTURE

You desire truth in the inward being;
therefore teach me wisdom in my secret heart.

—*Psalm 51:6 (NRSVUE)*

My husband and I enjoy many places in our community where we can walk. I especially love the wooded trails just minutes from where we live. Regardless of the season, the trees are our allies and secret keepers as we walk and talk together. It reminds me of the garden walks Adam and Eve took with God. They enjoyed an unforced relationship with God that we long for.

We can have the same intimate relationship. However, it must grow from honesty, vulnerability, and obedience. Developing intimacy with God is sometimes a painful learning curve. We aren't always honest with ourselves about our motives and perspectives. How can we be honest with God if we aren't honest with ourselves?

Too many times I have come to God upset about something or someone. What I wanted from God was agreement. Instead, I received his honesty about my motives, my closed mind, or my self-absorption. God shared honestly from a heart of love, and although I did not feel shame, I felt exposed in a way that I could recognize God was right. The more I accepted honesty from God, the more I wanted to give honesty back to him.

As God models honesty with us, we can learn how to be more honest with ourselves. It means we ask more questions of God rather than telling God what to do about something. Remember that God "will bring to light what is hidden in darkness and will expose the motives of the heart" (1 Corinthians 4:5a).

Anything but honesty is an unnecessary interchange with God. He already knows what's in our hearts anyway. Honesty with God brings new growth and self-awareness. Honesty with God makes us stronger, not weaker. It creates the closeness we crave. This is where we return to the walk in the garden with God, who never wants to find us hiding. He wants us to recognize what he knows about us and how he uses it to transform and protect us. All God needs from us is a spirit that seeks the truth and knows we will always find it in his loving words.

BURNING QUESTIONS

1. Where do you fear honesty with God or yourself?

____

____

____

____

____

____

2. How can you practice honesty with God today?

AFFIRMATION

As I learn to be more honest with God,
I will learn to be more honest with myself.

PRAYER FOR TODAY

God of all honesty, I need your honesty to
help me be more honest with myself and those I love.

FOURTH SUNDAY IN LENT

A BURNING LOVE

WORSHIP FOCUS

Come for Love

SCRIPTURE

And that you may love the LORD *your God,*
listen to his voice, and hold fast to him.

—*Deuteronomy 30:20a*

The Bible is a love story. It is the story of God's love with backbone, determination, persistence, and uncompromising boundaries for our protection. He does nothing without us in mind—and not just us from this generation. His actions and instructions are for all of us, from the beginning of time to the end of it on this earth. His love burns deeply for us. No one will ever love us more strongly, more purely, or more completely than God.

We bring our hearts to God for examination to hear from the One who loved us first. When we have a fresh encounter with the burning love of God, we have more love to share. This week, take the journey to review God's burning love for you and let his love set your heart burning for those who don't yet understand how much God loves them.

BURNING QUESTION

Which action do I need today in worship: loving, listening, or holding fast?

SUNDAY PRAYER

Great Lover of my soul, awaken my desire to recognize and receive more of your love so that I may listen more and obey quickly.

MONDAY

UNFAILING LOVE

SCRIPTURE

Many are the woes of the wicked, but the LORD's unfailing love surrounds the one who trusts in him.

—Psalm 32:10

God is not a stranger to our mishaps in love. He sees every rejection, every betrayal, every argument, every separation. He longs for us to know that he is the God of *unfailing* love. It's not just one of his traits; it's *the* trait that binds everything we know about God together. He loves deeply, with empowerment and healing, and his love does not fail. Ever.

It's time to stop wishing God would give us what we want and let God give us what we need—his unfailing love. He wants his love to be our first love because no other love can give us what God can give so completely. Who would we be if we completely believed in God's unfailing love? What would happen if we fully accepted that we are worth loving for eternity? Who could we become if we accepted how God values and believes in us? Wouldn't we live with more security and less fear? Wouldn't we reflect our original, God-given identity and stop chasing someone else's idea of who we should be?

Lent gives us space to review the loves in our lives that pull us down, frustrate us, or hurt us. Sometimes they are people; sometimes they are activities or habits. We can't always remove them, but we can, with God's love, reassign their priority in our lives. We can ask God to give us what we need to protect us from frustrating and self-destructive detours. We can receive *unfailing* love that empowers us to receive and give love from a healed place and not a wounded one.

Let God love you today. You—the needy, wanting-to-do-better you; the you who needs to know that when God loved the world, he directed that love personally and unfailingly to *you*. You are not just another prayer request. You are the apple of God's eye, God's treasure, God's reason for getting involved in the mess of this world.

Live knowing that the *unfailing* love of God is your armor, your home, and the lap of a doting father of a prized child. Live loved. Deeply loved.

BURNING QUESTIONS

1. Where do you feel the most unloved? Ask God to bring his unfailing love there.

____

____

____

____

____

____

____

2. Whom do you have trouble loving? Ask God to bring his unfailing love there.

AFFIRMATION

I am loved beyond my understanding, and I am also empowered to love others more with God's unfailing love.

PRAYER FOR TODAY

Compassionate Father, sometimes I feel under-loved because I don't allow you to love me with your unfailing love. Show me your love today.

TUESDAY

SCANDALOUS LOVE

SCRIPTURE

For God so loved the world that he gave his one and only Son, that whoever believes in him shall not perish but have eternal life.

—John 3:16

I feel like a pinpoint in the world whenever I find myself in an airplane flying over open land or cities. My larger-than-life world reduces me to ant status from this viewpoint. I echo David's cry, *Who am I that you pay attention to me?* (see Psalm 8:4).

But God paid attention to all of us when he sent Jesus. We practice the story without understanding the truly scandalous act of love this was. God—who has the power to destroy the unreceptive and the stubborn—acted in all love for every person born on this planet. Think about it. God gave his love away outrageously, generously, and selflessly when he sent us Jesus. And what happened? Jesus was rejected, despised, and crucified. It seems scandalous to give more love than you get back. But really, we are the scandalous ones—always loving with reserve, calculating our return, hoarding more than we give. That's not a picture of God's love.

A true encounter with God's great love changes us. His love transforms us from the inside out. Knowing that we are loved wholly by God because of who he created us to be, we are freed to love ourselves in healthy ways and love others in productive ways.

Are we ready for God's love to empower every loving thing we do? When God's love is our pivot point in relationships, we understand that loving God's way never empties us. His love fills us again and again. Scandalous, isn't it? And all God wants in exchange is first place in the loves of our lives. Can we give him what he wants the most? Aren't *we* the scandalous hoarders if we don't?

BURNING QUESTIONS

1. When has God's generous love supported you in the past when the way you tried to love didn't?

2. Whom could you love better if you loved with God's love?

AFFIRMATION

God loves me with a scandalous love that empowers me to love myself and others God's way.

PRAYER FOR TODAY

God of unfailing Love, help me look to you for love before I look anywhere else.

WEDNESDAY

DEEP AND WIDE

SCRIPTURE

And I pray that you, being rooted and established in love, may have power, together with all the Lord's holy people, to grasp how wide and long and high and deep is the love of Christ.

—Ephesians 3:17b–18

I've seen the Grand Canyon with its abyss where the river below looks more like a stream I could jump across. I sat on rocky ground with my tennis shoes staunch against a boulder because I knew I would not survive a fall into that crevice. It was immense but not limitless. As wide as an ocean is, as long as a journey around the sun might be, as high as a space launch might reach, and as deep as a volcano might go—God's love is wider, longer, higher, deeper.

I sit in my small corner of the world and cannot fully imagine the limitless reach of God's love. But I know this in the deepest way possible: God's love reaches me. His love reaches every hidden place where thoughts, hopes, dreams, and motives are born. He knows me from the inside out and loves me limitlessly.

I didn't always believe that. I remember a Bible teacher who counseled us to sit silently until we understood that God's love was enough for us at that moment and for that day. I completed that exercise every morning for several weeks. To focus on God's singular and comprehensive love for me was life-changing. From a place of being completely loved, I loved others better, more willingly, and without expecting anything in return.

Too many times we try to love on our own, when our love bank has been depleted. Instead, we must start with how much God loves us. We can't simply tuck this fact away in our heads. It must be a truth we experience, fresh with each sunrise. God always gives us enough love to love others. He knows where our love can make a difference. We follow God's leading because self-willed love is often self-serving.

Whom is God calling you to love? Don't love with your needy, self-protecting love. Love from a fresh awareness of God's wide, long, deep, and high love that replaces your best effort with his limitless love. Then you will discover that, the more you share God's love, the quicker your love bank gets refilled.

BURNING QUESTIONS

1. What is your biggest hurdle in believing in God's limitless love for you?

____

____

____

____

____

____

2. Where do you try to share *your* love instead of God's love? How can you change that today?

____

____

____

____

____

____

____

____

____

____

____

____

____

____

AFFIRMATION

I can share more love with family and friends when
I know how limitlessly loved by God I am.

PRAYER FOR TODAY

God of limitless love, remind me how your love heals
where I have been hurt or betrayed by others.

THURSDAY

HE TOOK MY CASE

SCRIPTURE

You, Lord, took up my case; you redeemed my life.

—Lamentations 3:58

As an awkward teenager, my mouth usually got me into more trouble than my actions did. I tended to argue a point to the despair of everyone else in my family. My sister used to take me aside and plead, "Why can't you just stop arguing and leave it alone?" I couldn't answer then, but I think I can now.

I wanted someone to stand up for me and take my side. I fought for self-worth that I thought someone else had to give me—preferably on a silver platter, and a trumpet would be nice! What I didn't understand was that what I wanted the most would never come from an argument; it would come because the Creator of this world stood up for me.

What God did for me, he did for the whole world. At just the right moment, God took our case. He opened his heart and showed us Jesus to help us know his love as the purest, most healing, most redeeming love ever shared. He knows our self-centered, sinful history, can see our future, and wants to love us into eternity with every good and perfect gift along the way.

God took our case and argued our worth by giving us Jesus. God willingly became human to experience rejection, betrayal, and humiliating death. His argument for us enables us to live deeply loved so that we can love others honestly and selflessly in ways that do not empty us. We can live with healed self-concepts birthed in God's love for us. We can live knowing someone is always standing up for us with an argument of love that no one can silence except ourselves.

Today is a good day to live in the love of the One who took our case to the cross. We can live loved, in order to love more fully. We can live loved, in order to serve without needing something in return. We can live loved, and enjoy the original intimacy model with God, without fear of anything he already knows. Why would we want to live any other way?

BURNING QUESTIONS

1. What difference does it make that Jesus carried your case to the cross?

____

____

____

____

____

____

____

2. What does Jesus deserve from you because he died to save you from living without God?

____

____

____

____

____

____

____

____

____

____

____

____

____

____

____

AFFIRMATION

Jesus took my case, and I need no other argument to know I am loved.

PRAYER FOR TODAY

Eternal Litigator, remind me how you stood up for me,
and help me stand up for you.

FRIDAY

THE SALT AND LIGHT EFFECT

SCRIPTURE

You are the salt of the earth. But if the salt loses its saltiness, how can it be made salty again? It is no longer good for anything, except to be thrown out and trampled underfoot. You are the light of the world. A town built on a hill cannot be hidden.

—Matthew 5:13–14

The TV commercial for a popular salted chip brags that you can't eat just one. Salt creates an appetite for more. Is that why Jesus used salt to remind us how to live our lives to help people develop an appetite for God? It's the salty-chip response. We are to be God's bag of salty chips for the world around us. Will our neighbors—the soccer family we see at games, people we get to know at the gym—get a taste of God's love by interacting with us?

And what did Jesus say would happen if we lost our saltiness? We would get trampled. Have you been feeling a little trampled in this world? If so, could there be a connection with our lack of saltiness?

In case we didn't get the message, Jesus went on to talk about the light effect. We know that we need light to see. But Jesus wasn't telling us to carry flashlights or pay our electric bill. He wants us to make sure the light of God lives in us. This is light that needs no words to be recognized.

Don't misunderstand here. This isn't a vote for a silent witness. This verse reminds us to keep God's light in our lives with our words, attitudes, and perspectives—not by pointing our fingers and using words that repel, divide, or destroy people. We need words of light that speak the truth in love.

The world is filled with bland and dark lives. We are called to be salted people with light that shines out in every way possible. It is a counter-cultural way to live, that's for sure. But it can't be artificial. We begin with more of God in us. We look for his light wherever we experience darkness.

Jesus living *in* us is the hope of this world. But it will take a lot more salt and light. Are we up for the challenge?

BURNING QUESTIONS

1. How can you monitor the saltiness of your Christian witness? What would make you saltier?

____

____

____

____

____

____

____

2. Who needs you to be God's light in their darkness?

AFFIRMATION

The closer I walk with Jesus, the more of his salt and light I can share.

PRAYER FOR TODAY

Holy Lord, help me exchange my complaints about this world for more salt and light that I can share to make a difference your way!

SATURDAY

PRAYING WE

SCRIPTURE

So I turned to the Lord God and pleaded with him in prayer and petition . . . and confessed . . . we have sinned and done wrong

—Daniel 9:3a, 4a, 5a

Our worldview changes when God's unfailing and scandalous love permeates our hearts. We take God's perspective. There is no *them* and *us*. We all need God's forgiveness. That's where Daniel's prayer for his people is a good model for praying for our community, nation, and world. Daniel prayed *we*. Daniel became a representative of his wayward people and confessed not just his own sins but all of their sins. This is intercessory prayer at its deepest level. However, praying *we* isn't for the faint of heart.

We live among many who do not understand God's unfailing love. We live among people who consider God's laws to be narrow-minded and restrictive. They refuse anyone who would dictate morality, for fear they might lose their autonomy. Daniel lived with the same kind of people. He didn't talk *against* them; he prayed *for* them and confessed their brokenness as his own.

We need more people like Daniel who will carry the subtle and blatant ways people have turned away from God and his Word.

We have sinned as a group. *We* have sinned as a neighborhood. *We* have sinned as a church. *We* have lived for ourselves. *We* have tried to fit into our culture. *We* have run after other gods. *We* have participated in actions that make it difficult for people to see the glory of God living in us and among us. Therefore, *we* must confess.

If we prayed Daniel's prayer, we would share the suffering that took Christ to the cross to die for people who do not love him or understand his love. We pray this way if we want God to use us as magnets and transformational examples for anyone who is confused about who God is. Until sin breaks us wherever we see it, until we stop talking about *them* and start praying about *us*, the awakening God wants to bring won't come.

Today, learn to pray *we* from the burning in your heart that only God can ignite.

BURNING QUESTIONS

1. How can you pray Daniel's prayer for your community?

____

____

____

____

____

____

____

____

2. How does praying *we* change your attitude toward people who live against God's love and life?

AFFIRMATION

What breaks God's heart breaks mine and compels me to pray we.

PRAYER FOR TODAY

Lord of all, help me pray more we prayers and become an agent of healing in this mixed-up world.

FIFTH SUNDAY IN LENT

BURNING ENCOUNTERS WITH JESUS

WORSHIP FOCUS

Responding

SCRIPTURE

My heart has heard you say, "Come and talk with me."
And my heart responds, "LORD, I am coming."

—Psalm 27:8 (NLT)

The more self-sufficient we think we are, the more we fool ourselves. We are needy people. Perhaps that's why the extravagance of God sometimes feels unrealistic or out of our reach.

This week, we will review encounters people had with Jesus. Each story is part of our own story and will help us uncover needs we have not recognized or that we have tried to meet our own way.

It is time to take a lighter journey to the cross by leaving behind what we don't need and receiving from God what we do.

BURNING QUESTION

How will you prepare to encounter Jesus today?

____

____

____

____

____

____

____

____

____

____

____

____

____

SUNDAY PRAYER

Gracious God, burn away what doesn't belong in my heart to prepare me for a fresh encounter with you.

MONDAY

THE TAX COLLECTOR IN ME

SCRIPTURE

After this, Jesus went out and saw a tax collector by the name of Levi sitting at his tax booth. "Follow me," Jesus said to him, and Levi got up, left everything and followed him.

—Luke 5:27–28

Jesus's disciple whom we know as Matthew—called Levi in this passage from Luke—was a tax collector. He was hated, snubbed, and considered to be a Jewish traitor. He over-collected Roman taxes with no remorse. Numbed to his social isolation because he lived well, he probably rationalized his actions with gray-area thinking. Did he believe Rome owed him? Or maybe he thought he was doing it for his family. We can always find a reason to do what we want.

What disarming look did Jesus give him? What made Matthew see the contrast between the lie he built his life upon and the truth that could free him? What made him leave his tax-collecting post and follow the teacher who saw into his heart? It was love—a love so great and permeating that Matthew's life completely changed. He no longer desired to take from others. Instead, he lived to give more than he took.

Sometimes our insecurities push us into tax-collecting ways. We expect others to give us the confidence, the understanding, the security we need. We can take our tax-collecting postures until Jesus looks us in the face. He reminds us that when we let others supply what should come first from him, we stay needy. We have the same opportunity Jesus gave Matthew. We can leave our tax-collecting folly to follow him into a deeper security we can't know any other way.

BURNING QUESTIONS

1. Where do you take more than you give?

2. What do you need to leave behind in order to follow Jesus today?

AFFIRMATION

When I am in need, Jesus is my first responder.

PRAYER FOR TODAY

Promise-keeping Lord, protect me from taking from others what you have promised to give more generously.

TUESDAY

RICH OR POOR?

SCRIPTURE

Just then a man came up to Jesus and asked, "Teacher, what good thing must I do to get eternal life?"

—Matthew 19:16

Jesus was on his way to Jerusalem when he was interrupted. Not one to ignore a person, Jesus stopped and directed his attention to the wealthy man. When this intruder had Jesus's attention, he called Jesus "teacher." Clearly this man had already heard enough about Jesus to know that if anyone could answer his burning question, Jesus could. So, he asked. He was looking for a kind of security he did not get from money or status.

Aren't we all? We grab what we think will secure us—the next promotion, investment, relationship, or some other opportunity that promises more than we currently have (and usually more than it can actually provide). Here is where our perception of security is flawed, just like this man's.

Jesus pointed the man to God's commandments. "Which ones?" the man asked (v. 18). His response showed his ignorance. He wanted to be sure he obeyed only the right commandments that would secure his eternal life—as if he could pick and choose his obedience.

Jesus didn't let him play word games. Instead, he tested his desperation, telling him to sell his possessions, give to the poor, and follow Jesus. It was a chance for this supposedly rich man to live with less while experiencing more. However, because he had "great wealth" (v. 22) and was apparently unwilling to give it up, he left Jesus's presence feeling sadder than ever.

We point fingers at this man for his foolishness, but we should be pointing at ourselves. What is something Jesus has asked us to surrender that we questioned or refused? What are we supposed to learn from this story? Perhaps we should remember that every good and perfect gift comes from God (James 1:17). What God gives us, he also helps us use most effectively. Less *is* more when God is in charge. Let God prove it.

BURNING QUESTIONS

1. How do you demonstrate that everything you have and value is a gift from God?

____

____

____

____

____

____

____

____

____

2. If God reveals what you hold too tightly, how will you let God show you where it belongs?

AFFIRMATION

Every good and perfect gift is from God above! (See James 1:17.)

PRAYER FOR TODAY

Wise Giver, help me be open to your gifts and practice obedience about where they belong in my life.

WEDNESDAY

ONE OF TEN

SCRIPTURE

Now on his way to Jerusalem, Jesus traveled along the border between Samaria and Galilee. As he was going into a village, ten men who had leprosy met him. They stood at a distance and called out in a loud voice, "Jesus, Master, have pity on us!"

—Luke 17:11–13

By this time in Jesus's ministry, interruptions weren't new. He was no longer nameless or unrecognizable. Crowds followed him. He was a magnet for the sick and disabled, so there was nothing unusual about ten lepers respectfully keeping their distance yet crying out to him for help. Pity isn't much help, but maybe it was all they felt capable of asking for. Leprosy made them outcasts, robbing them of family, worship, and identity. Leprosy gave them no rights in the community.

In this encounter, Jesus didn't touch the lepers. He didn't even pronounce them healed. He only instructed them to go see the priests. It meant another journey, but they obeyed, and on their way to see the priests, they noticed that their flesh-eating sores disappeared. They were healed! Each man experienced life-changing healing that would allow them to return to their families and normalcy—but only one returned to Jesus to say thank you (vv. 15–16).

The point of this story is not the healing; it is the gratitude. And the question we must ask of ourselves is whether we would have returned to Jesus to say thank you. Where does gratitude live in our relationship with Jesus? Are we always asking for more of something we think will make a difference? Are we takers or thankers?

If gratitude ruled our lives, no one would suffer in silence because grateful people would notice and help. Every child would know love, and every home would be safe. Work would be a joy, not a taskmaster. We would live in God's blessing, and the end of life on earth would be more of a benediction. If only gratitude ruled the world!

We can change that by practicing gratitude today. Don't let a good gift pass by without saying thank you to God. The man who came back to say thank you to Jesus went away with more than physical healing. What waits for us if we practice more gratitude?

BURNING QUESTIONS

1. When have you held back your gratitude until you had the answer from Jesus you wanted?

____

____

____

____

____

____

____

2. How can you make gratitude your first response today?

AFFIRMATION

I am not self-made or self-powered.
Everything is a gift, and I will live with gratitude.

PRAYER FOR TODAY

Awesome Father, with all my heart I say thank you. Help me live my gratitude.

THURSDAY

DEAD MAN WALKING

SCRIPTURE

When he had said this, Jesus called in a loud voice, "Lazarus, come out!" The dead man came out, his hands and feet wrapped with strips of linen, and a cloth around his face. Jesus said to them, "Take off the grave clothes and let him go."

—John 11:43–44

The story of Lazarus is a personal and dramatic healing by Jesus. Lazarus was dead for three days. They wrapped him in burial strips and had every reason to believe rigor mortis had set in. We know that Mary and Martha, Lazarus's sisters, were unhappy about Jesus's delay. They knew Jesus could have healed his illness, but three days dead in the tomb made them believe it was too late.

Maybe that's the first lesson from this story: it is *never* too late for Jesus to make a difference. Not in illness, marriage, work, or anything that feels hopeless. But there is a companion lesson too: don't try to tell Jesus what he could have done better!

In this grief-filled scene, Jesus shared a sentiment we don't see in other stories. He cried. I don't believe his tears were about what could have happened or even the three-day agony his friends had endured. His tears went deeper as he experienced the tug-of-war between the confines of humanity and the unfailing love of his Father. With a startling shout, he called Lazarus out of the tomb with the authority of heaven. The call woke Lazarus, restarted his heart, returned his blood flow, and removed all evidence of physical death except for the grave clothes he'd been wrapped in. It must have been frightening to see Lazarus shuffle out of the tomb—even more frightening when Jesus instructed people to remove the binding cloths.

We live bound up too—not with grave clothes but with pressures that could take us to the grave before our time. We live restricted in ways Jesus never wanted. We point fingers and share Martha's accusation, "If you had been there."

Instead, we need to hear the life-giving call to leave behind what keeps us from life *in* Christ, *for* him, and *with* him. I'm not sure we're ready for resurrection truth unless we hear Jesus's call to Lazarus as his call to us as well. Don't pass this story too quickly without asking what has bound you. Perhaps if we sit listening long enough, we will hear Jesus's compassionate and life-giving invitation to us: "Come out!" Then we will be ready to live resurrection truth.

BURNING QUESTIONS

1. What binds you today or in this season of life?

____

____

____

2. How can you obey Jesus's call to *come out* and live in his way?

AFFIRMATION

Jesus demonstrated power that I can live in today.

PRAYER FOR TODAY

Powerful Lord, when you call me, I will come out of what has bound me.

FRIDAY

USEFUL WASTE

SCRIPTURE

Then Mary took about a pint of pure nard, an expensive perfume; she poured it on Jesus' feet and wiped his feet with her hair. And the house was filled with the fragrance of the perfume. But one of his disciples, Judas Iscariot, who was later to betray him, objected, "Why wasn't this perfume sold and the money given to the poor? It was worth a year's wages."

—John 12:3–5

Jesus and his disciples enjoyed leisure time at the home of Lazarus after Jesus brought him back to life. Mary entered with a jar and stood behind Jesus, who reclined at the table. Before anyone noticed, she broke the jar and poured the expensive oil on Jesus's head. Confusion settled in the group. Judas believed she was wasting expensive oil that could have been sold to help the poor.

Before you point a finger, think about taking a year's worth of your take-home pay and splurging on a thank-you gift for the surgeon who saved your loved one's life. Would it be irresponsible or generous? The problem is that there is no formula here. However, we do have Jesus's response, which indicates that he thought she had done a beautiful thing.

The story reminds us that there is a time when waste is generous and hoarding is closed-hearted. There is a time when pouring it on is better than giving up merely a drop or two. There is a time when monetary value is irrelevant and only the heart can measure the gift.

Whom would we have been in this scene? One of the indignant witnesses who saw the waste? One of the quiet ones waiting for Jesus's response? Or someone who wished they had thought of doing such a beautiful thing?

Jesus's teaching here is that we will lose what we hold too tightly and gain what we think we have given up. It is the practice of useful waste. Sometimes useful waste is playing with your children instead of trying to get ahead on bills, groceries, or maintenance projects. Sometimes useful waste drops everything when a neighbor needs a ride to the doctor. We can't choose opportunities for useful waste; they choose us.

Jesus reminds us that what we do for others in these unexpected moments, we do for him. We anoint him with the oil of thanksgiving for what he has brought to our lives. We follow him to the cross, where there is no place for our will to take priority. It is useful waste, and to Jesus, it will always be a beautiful gift.

BURNING QUESTIONS

1. Who are you in this scene: the one who practices useful waste or the one who criticizes it?

___

___

___

___

2. How can you live more generously with your time, money, skill, or energy?

AFFIRMATION

The more I acknowledge Jesus's generosity toward me, the more I want to be generous to others.

PRAYER FOR TODAY

Merciful Lord, teach me where I can give more love, forgiveness, and second chances in the extravagant ways you continue to give them to me.

SATURDAY

WILL YOU REALLY LAY DOWN YOUR LIFE?

SCRIPTURE

Peter asked, "Lord, why can't I follow you now? I will lay down my life for you."

—John 13:37

Jesus knew his time with the disciples was limited. He did not waste words as he spoke about going where they could not go (see John 13:33). What waited for Jesus and his followers wouldn't be easy, and Jesus wanted to prepare them.

Bumbling Peter tried to prove his allegiance by promising, "I will lay down my life for you." We stand there with Peter and want to say the same. However, like Peter, we don't always understand what it will take. Laying down our lives for Jesus is not simply a promise to stand up for Jesus in a cultural conflict. It is about laying down our will and right to control our own lives. This laying down of our lives doesn't begin in the big moments. It starts with the little ones. It starts with the words we use, the motives we act on, the priorities we choose, and the rights we protect.

I like the way The Message paraphrases the laying-down invitation in Romans12:1: "So here's what I want you to do, God helping you: Take your everyday, ordinary life—your sleeping, eating, going-to-work, and walking-around life—and place it before God as an offering." Now that's a lay-down for sure. No strings attached. *Here I am, Lord! Use me, move me, or tell me to stay.*

If we learn to lay down our lives in small ways, we won't know any other way to live when a crisis comes. We won't miss the moment that holds more eternity than we imagined because we will already be in laying-down mode.

We can't brush Peter's boast away without recognizing where we have made our own empty promises. But we can start with the simple moments and learn what happens when we give them to Jesus without our expectations connected. Hear the question again: *Will you really lay down your life?* How are you answering it today?

BURNING QUESTIONS

1. How will you lay down your words and actions before Jesus without claiming your rights to them?

____

____

____

____

____

____

____

2. What has Jesus taught you about laying down your life that has grown your faith?

AFFIRMATION

I will surrender what Jesus points out to prepare me for whatever Jesus directs.

PRAYER FOR TODAY

Life-giving Jesus, because you laid down your life for me,
I have every good reason to lay down mine for you.

SIXTH SUNDAY IN LENT (PALM SUNDAY)

A HEART THAT BURNS

WORSHIP FOCUS

Remember

SCRIPTURE

Rejoice greatly, Daughter Zion! Shout, Daughter Jerusalem! See, your king comes to you, righteous and victorious, lowly and riding on a donkey, on a colt, the foal of a donkey.

—Zechariah 9:9

We look at the last week of Jesus's life before the cross. We know that everything he says and does carries weight. This is not the time for the trivial and mundane.

Each day we must continue to look for how our commitment and obedience will help us grasp what Jesus's death on the cross means. We must ask ourselves if our hearts burn with what carried Jesus to the cross. We cannot only review how this event changed the world. We must also ask how it reorients our own lives. How does it share hope, no matter where we find chaos or conflict?

Ask Jesus to guide you as you take these questions into this week. Let him confirm new understandings and show you how to live new insights. No matter how often we have reviewed this story, we need a new surrender to what Jesus did and why.

BURNING QUESTION

What difference has it made that Jesus brought salvation that you cannot negotiate or reproduce?

____

____

____

____

____

____

____

____

____

SUNDAY PRAYER

Life-giving Jesus, help me review the events of Holy Week to rekindle and sustain a consuming fire in my heart for all that you want me to live because of the cross.

MONDAY OF HOLY WEEK

ARE WE PALM SUNDAY PEOPLE?

SCRIPTURE

In your relationships with one another, have the same mindset as Christ Jesus.

—Philippians 2:5

Jerusalem was crowded with people shouting a hopeful song. Were they celebrating Jesus as one who was *like* a Messiah, or did they understand that Jesus *was* the Messiah? Palm Sunday won't answer that question. The answer comes with what they did with their praise on Monday. We know what happened on Monday. They put away their praise palms and returned to life as usual.

Are we Palm Sunday people? Are we content to join the crowd on Sunday and sing our praise, only to turn back to our week without living out the truth we praised?

We must change the story. We must be the same praising people on Monday. We must turn deaf ears to half-truths and twisted arguments. We must raise our voices for Jesus in our family and work relationships. We must take our Sunday praise to the places where people suffer, struggle, protest, and bury dreams. We must see Jesus riding into our days and join the angels who sang at his birth, "Glory in the highest . . . Peace has come!"

We must live as people whose Sunday praise is as vibrant and magnetic on Monday as it is on Sunday. Our world needs us to be more than Palm Sunday people. Let's surprise them and live our praise the rest of the week.

BURNING QUESTIONS

1. Whom would you have been in the Palm Sunday gathering, and why would you have joined the parade?

2. What difference does Sunday praise make on your Monday morning?

AFFIRMATION

I have every reason to join the praise of Palm Sunday and even more reasons to keep living it on Monday!

PRAYER FOR TODAY

Worthy Christ, may the words of my mouth and the meditations of my heart lead me to keep praising who you are and what you have done.

TUESDAY OF HOLY WEEK

WHEN JESUS TURNED THE TABLES

SCRIPTURE

For we are the temple of the living God.

—2 Corinthians 6:16b

When I was six or seven years old, my father pastored a small church. There was no money for janitorial services. On Saturday nights our family cleaned the church. While I didn't always enjoy it, there was something special about getting the building ready for Sunday. It was a feeling I've never forgotten. One of the lessons I learned was that it was always worth getting ready for God to do his work.

What did Jesus see when he walked into the temple and turned over the tables of the money changers? Did he see entrepreneurs trying to capitalize on religious needs? Did he see selfish greed masked as ministry? Something was wrong, and Jesus was having none of it. Jesus called for his Father's place of worship to stop peddling religion and make every square inch a place where people and God could connect easily, intimately, and with transformation.

Today we must remember that we are God's temple. We are the living stones that God wants to use to raise a people who share God's light in our dark world. Sometimes we need a few tables turned over in our hearts. We know we carry too much unnecessarily. We crowd out the work Jesus wants to do in our temple hearts.

The temple-cleansing story is not only about the people who misuse God's house. The story also reminds us that Jesus wants to clean our hearts from unnecessary work and worries that will not grow or produce God's fruit. We must welcome his work to edit our thoughts, perspectives, and priorities. How would Jesus respond if we let him?

I don't think Jesus left the temple angry that day. I believe he left broken-hearted. Did anyone understand his message? Did anyone change? Probably not the money changers, who likely took their broken tables home to repair them for another day. Let's not be like them—more upset about how Jesus messes with our plans than we are about realizing we have failed to learn and do what he wants. Let's determine to accept any table-turning that Jesus asks us to do.

BURNING QUESTIONS

1. What table does Jesus want to overturn in your heart to get more of your attention?

____

____

____

____

2. How can you be a worshiper who makes God's house a house of prayer?

AFFIRMATION

I am God's temple, and Jesus has my permission to clean it.

PRAYER FOR TODAY

Freeing Lord, my heart is an over-crowded closet. Help me reduce the clutter.

WEDNESDAY OF HOLY WEEK

AM I AN ANSWER TO JESUS'S PRAYER?

SCRIPTURE

I will remain in the world no longer, but they are still in the world, and I am coming to you. Holy Father, protect them by the power of your name, the name you gave me, so that they may be one as we are one.

—John 17:11

Have you ever heard someone pray for you who did not know you were listening? The closest I ever came was seeing my name written in my mother's Bible with a date. I knew my mother prayed for me and, because I recognized the date, I knew how God answered her prayer.

Printed on the pages of our Bibles, captured for us in black and white, we can eavesdrop on the prayer Jesus prayed for us before he went to the cross. Think about it. Before Jesus paid the price as our sacrificed lamb to take away our sins and return us to the loving arms of our Creator, Jesus carried us to his Father's heart.

Before anything else, Jesus prayed for our unity (vv. 20–21). He asked his Father to help us establish oneness so deep and unbreakable that the world would know us by our unity instead of our protests (v. 21). He didn't only want us to be one with each other; he also prayed for oneness with God that would mirror the relationship of Jesus with his Father (vv. 20–21). He prayed fervently that the world would come to know who he was and what he came to do because of the way his followers understood and carried out his mission (v. 23).

Are we living answers to this personal and intimate prayer of Jesus? Each part of Jesus's prayer shares a sobering question we must answer before we take our places before the cross on Good Friday. Jesus didn't die for our excuses or complacency; he died for every way we have rejected or replaced God's ways. The call of the cross comes to us through Jesus's prayer. Ultimately, we must answer whether it has become our prayer as well.

BURNING QUESTIONS

1. How are you answering Jesus's prayer for you and your faith community?

2. How can you address any areas where you are not an answer to Jesus's prayer but want to be?

AFFIRMATION

The more I am one with Jesus and his purpose, the more I participate in the unity he prayed for.

PRAYER FOR TODAY

Sovereign Lord, I want to be an answer to your prayer for unity. Show me where to begin.

MAUNDY THURSDAY

SEEDS OF BETRAYAL

SCRIPTURE

Greatly distressed, each one asked in turn, "Am I the one, Lord?"

—Matthew 26:22 (NLT)

Betrayal is a subtle visitor—until it isn't. On the night Jesus was betrayed, only he saw the darkness lurking. He gathered with his disciples to eat the Passover meal. Jesus always used every moment to open hearts to the truth. He took the towel and basin and washed his disciples' feet. Peter, outspoken as always, protested the inappropriateness of his Master acting like a servant. Jesus looked into Peter's eyes and helped him realize this washing was not just about dirty feet. It was an invitation to surrender more of Peter's raw and misguided enthusiasm.

Judas was also there with dirty feet and misguided assumptions. Jesus gave Judas the same opportunity for surrender that he gave the other disciples. However, seeds of betrayal had already been growing. We saw them at Mary and Martha's house when Mary washed Jesus's feet with expensive perfume and Judas called it waste. It was betrayal hidden behind logic and reason.

We also must ask what seeds of betrayal might be buried in our own lives. Where do we use logic to identify mission and ministry? Where do our needs or insecurities betray the call of Jesus? Where do we follow him with reticence? Where have we allowed Jesus to wash our feet but not our hopes and dreams? A heart that burns for Jesus willingly and honestly allows Jesus to bring any hint of betrayal to the surface, where we can reject it. The issue isn't ranking its severity; the issue is rejecting the seed so it does not grow.

We don't usually put ourselves in the same category as Judas. However, his betrayal didn't start on the night of Passover. It started with an attitude, an interpretation, a rationalization, and many secrets.

The important question we ask as we journey toward the cross is whose response we will choose—Peter's surrender or Judas's betrayal. Unlike Judas, we still have time to choose surrender.

BURNING QUESTIONS

1. Where do you resist Jesus's call to surrender, and how is that a form of betrayal?

____

____

____

____

____

____

____

2. Where are you vulnerable to developing a seed of betrayal, and how can you eliminate it?

AFFIRMATION

I refuse to grow a seed of betrayal because betrayal ultimately turns on me.

PRAYER FOR TODAY

Faithful Lord, may my obedience demonstrate a disgust for betraying you in any way.

GOOD FRIDAY

WHY, GOD?

SCRIPTURE

About three in the afternoon Jesus cried out in a loud voice, "Eli, Eli, lema sabachthani?" (which means "My God, my God, why have you forsaken me?").

—Matthew 27:46

We prefer our saviors to look like saviors. We echo Eugene Peterson's paraphrase of the first verse of Isaiah's great prophecy: "Who would have thought GOD's saving power would look like this?" (Isaiah 53:1, MSG). We look with disgust at images of Jesus nailed to a cross, the crown of thorns pressed into his forehead deep enough for blood to stream down his face, which is swollen from the abusive blows that had nothing to do with justice. He slumps, shoulders bowed, gasping for breath. And he says nothing.

He is the teacher who spoke with authority. His words delivered people from blindness, paralysis, death, and hopelessness. He commanded the wind and demons. But when he is the victim of injustice—he says nothing.

Our senses aren't prepared to see anyone nailed to wood, suffocating on a cross, losing blood, dehydrating, gasping for air with painful, inefficient results. Yet we can't take our eyes off Jesus. We must look. That's when we hear the cry that cuts us to the bone—words of utter abandonment. "My God, my God, why have you forsaken me?" Here is the *dark night of the soul.* The comfort and assurance Jesus needed before his last breath was not there. It made the darkness even darker.

But here also is where we realize what Jesus did for us and how far he went to do it. Jesus carried the sin of the world and took on the full effects of God's unrelenting repulsion of sin. In that moment, Jesus took what we need never experience—the total turning away of God from sin. In this moment, the heavens did not open. The dove did not descend. There was no voice affirming the Son who did what his Father asked. There was nothing but silence, darkness, and absence magnifying the agony of Jesus in ways we can never truly understand.

But don't stop looking—because here is where Jesus does the unbelievable. Jesus does not rail against what his Father did not do (save him from this pain). Jesus takes the darkness of God's absence and uses his last breath to commit himself into his Father's hands anyway.

I have heard the cries of many who blame God for not doing something. The darkness they live with is painful. But God does not withdraw his presence from us—not since Jesus took that darkness for us. We never need to know a single moment of abandonment in the way that Jesus experienced it.

So what will we do as we stand before the cross this Good Friday? Will we take all the whys we've hurled at God and leave them where Jesus did—in God's hands?

Since today is a solemn day of reflection, consider praying this prayer several times today:

Understanding Lord,

You know the whys I've lived unsuccessfully.

Today I stand before the cross

Where Jesus took the full impact of my sin.

How can I be anything but grateful?

Because of what you did for me,

I place my unanswered questions in your hands

Because keeping them will destroy me.

I confess that living without your presence

Is worse than living without the answers I want.

Today, I begin a new journey.

I will seek my answers

In the answer you gave all of us

Through the cross where you surrendered all,

Even your why.

Amen

HOLY SATURDAY

WAITING IN THE DARK

SCRIPTURE

Now the earth was formless and empty, darkness was over the surface of the deep, and the Spirit of God was hovering over the waters.

—Genesis 1:2

It was now about noon, and darkness came over the whole land until three in the afternoon, for the sun stopped shining. And the curtain of the temple was torn in two.

—Luke 23:44–45

Darkness is our enemy when it comes out of order and unexpectedly. A power outage that wipes out electricity and our quick access to light makes us feel helpless and vulnerable. We arm ourselves with flashlights and candles and wait for the light to return. This is the picture of Saturday's vigil following Friday's crucifixion. People went home, lost in a darkness they had not expected. The hope that had walked into their world as a person who healed and taught and stood up to Jewish leaders was dead. Darkness covered their lives as never before. It was the darkness of questions without answers, the darkness of absent hope, the darkness that made normal impossible—maybe forever. They did not expect the light to come on again.

It was like the darkness that covered the earth before the beginning of creation. That darkness was a void and an emptiness so thick and pervasive that nothing else existed. That darkness covered the earth and was the sum and substance of everything. In this dark beginning before our world came to be, God stepped in and created what had not existed: light. In a similar act of creation, God was about to do something with the darkness of this Saturday that would forever become a dividing line. It would either give us something to believe or something to reject.

It is hard to know how the disciples felt and what questions they asked on this day of darkness. More than one probably hurled an accusation into God's face. Others grieved what was lost. We want to tell them that God was bringing light that would be as dramatic and miraculous as the light of creation. We want to give them hope for what is coming. Yet what do we do in the dark times we encounter? We need to remember that darkness is never God's last word. Nothing is so hopeless that God cannot use it as raw material to make something new.

Today we sit in darkness, but we sit with hope because we know Light will come.

BURNING QUESTIONS

1. Where are you afraid that some darkness in your life is here to stay?

___

___

2. How has God brought light to a past darkness of yours, and what hope does that give you for a dark time now or in the future?

AFFIRMATION

If I persevere, I will see God turn my darkness into light.

PRAYER FOR TODAY

Creator of light, give me patience to wait for the light you will bring to my darkness.

EASTER SUNDAY

TAKE ANOTHER LOOK

SCRIPTURE

He is not here; he has risen, just as he said.
Come and see the place where he lay.

—Matthew 28:6

The sun rose on Sunday after Sabbath, just as it did every Sunday. But something was different today. The world changed, and the witnesses to the change each saw something different.

Think about the soldiers who drew the short end of the stick for all-night duty. They guarded a tomb to keep people from getting inside. They never expected that they needed to guard the tomb to keep someone from getting out!

Think about the women on their early-morning trek. They wanted to prepare the body of Jesus as a last way to honor the one they loved. They didn't know they had been invited to a welcome-back party.

Think about Peter and John running to the tomb with anger and disbelief boiling as they tried to make sense of what the women had reported—that Jesus's body was not in the tomb, that he was alive. They would take no one's word for it, but they never expected to be able to confirm what the women told them.

And what of us this Easter? What do we expect as we celebrate the story we know so well? What do we expect because we know the tomb is empty? That is the Easter question we must answer.

God wants us to see the full force of his power to change the end of our story. What could have happened didn't happen because God showed up! Every day beyond Easter is a day of empty-tomb discovery, a day we can find out how God wants to change the end of our story. Every day that we wake up, the empty tomb reminds us again that God works behind the scenes.

Today is a day to leave death clothes in an empty tomb and rediscover how the resurrection changes our story with more victory than defeat. Today, we look inside the empty tomb and leave our emptiness there too. We dare to believe that Jesus gives us whatever we need to live his way. Take another look at the empty tomb. What does God want us to know? When he speaks we will find the rest of our story.

BURNING QUESTIONS

1. Which of the first witnesses to the Easter miracle are you most like?

____

____

____

____

2. How will you keep Easter truth burning in your heart?

AFFIRMATION

Easter proves that I can live in the same power that raised Jesus from the dead.

PRAYER FOR TODAY

Risen Lord, help me live out the full meaning of
your resurrection in the coming year.

CONCLUSION

NO MORE LOCKED ROOMS

SCRIPTURE

Now that you know these things, God will bless you for doing them.

—John 13:17 (NLT)

Jesus appeared to his disciples several times after his resurrection. At least two of those times, the disciples locked themselves in a room for protection. They knew that the Jewish leaders wanted them dead. They had been marked as subversives who were threats to Jewish tradition just as Jesus had been. They still lived more afraid of what was outside instead of more confident in who had called them.

Where do we cower behind our own version of locked doors on this day after Easter Sunday? The climate in our communities isn't always kind to Christians. Like the disciples, we are also afraid to speak up, for fear of retribution. So what does the resurrection of Christ mean to people who live afraid of put-downs and rejection?

First, it means that nothing keeps Jesus away from his disciples. Can you imagine the disciples' surprise when Jesus appeared inside their locked room? Isn't that a bold reminder we need in these days of cultural chaos? Jesus is present. No angry mob, threat, or locked doors can keep him away. He knows how to come to where we are sitting in fear.

The second reminder is what Jesus brings when he comes. He brings peace. He brings his recognizable, saturating, present peace. This peace is a person, not a feeling. This peace is our victor, our defense, and our security. This peace goes with us wherever we go. Christ himself woos us out of our locked rooms to be representatives and spreaders of his peace. His peace shares forgiveness, reconciliation, and compassion. It shares strength, commitment, and perseverance as we live in resurrection power, not locked-room fear.

Are we bolder because of our journey to the cross? Is there an unquenchable fire in our hearts to live and share who Jesus is as we talk, connect, question, and love? As we transition into living the lessons we have learned from this journey, may we live them with the humility we learn from Jesus, who grabbed the towel and basin but never traded on his right to be served. May we live so closely connected to his peace that it becomes the first quality people notice about our lives. May we never confuse protest with proclamation. May we become the people of the resurrection because too many people around us are living dead, and Jesus wants to raise them to life too.

It is a bold and humbling mission. But people who follow the resurrected Christ will always find the empowerment they need to meet the challenge. Then none of us will need to cower behind locked doors.

PRAYER FOR THE YEAR AHEAD

Resurrected Lord,

Make me resurrection strong,

Empowered to live the fleshed-out Word of God.

I want to be your salt and light

Spreading forgiveness as generously as you did.

I want my life to burn into a flame for you

That turns to ash whatever I do not need

To live as your servant.

With this new look into the empty tomb

I face my broken world

To share this consuming fire in my heart

with whoever you bring my way.

Show me where to start

And how to keep burning for you.

Amen!

NOTES

www.ingramcontent.com/pod-product-compliance
Lightning Source LLC
LaVergne TN
LVHW051556080426
835510LV00020B/3009